THE
NATIVE AMERICANS
OF TEXAS

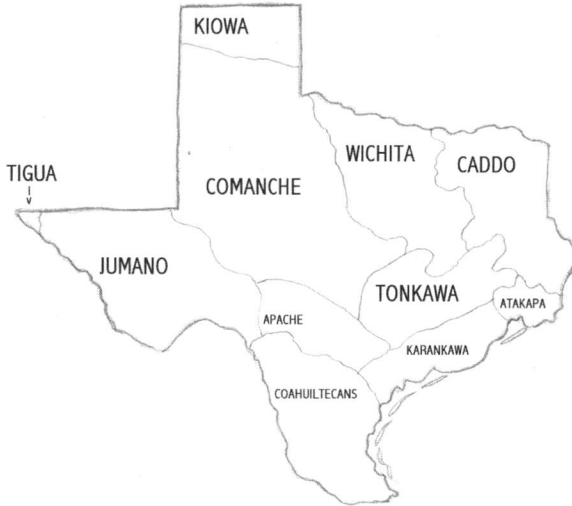

KIOWA

TIGUA

WICHITA   CADDO

COMANCHE

JUMANO

TONKAWA

ATAKAPA

APACHE

KARANKAWA

COAHUILTECANS

GRACE STAMPER

HENDRICK-LONG PUBLISHING CO. • HOUSTON

For my son,

Christopher

The Native Americans of Texas Map

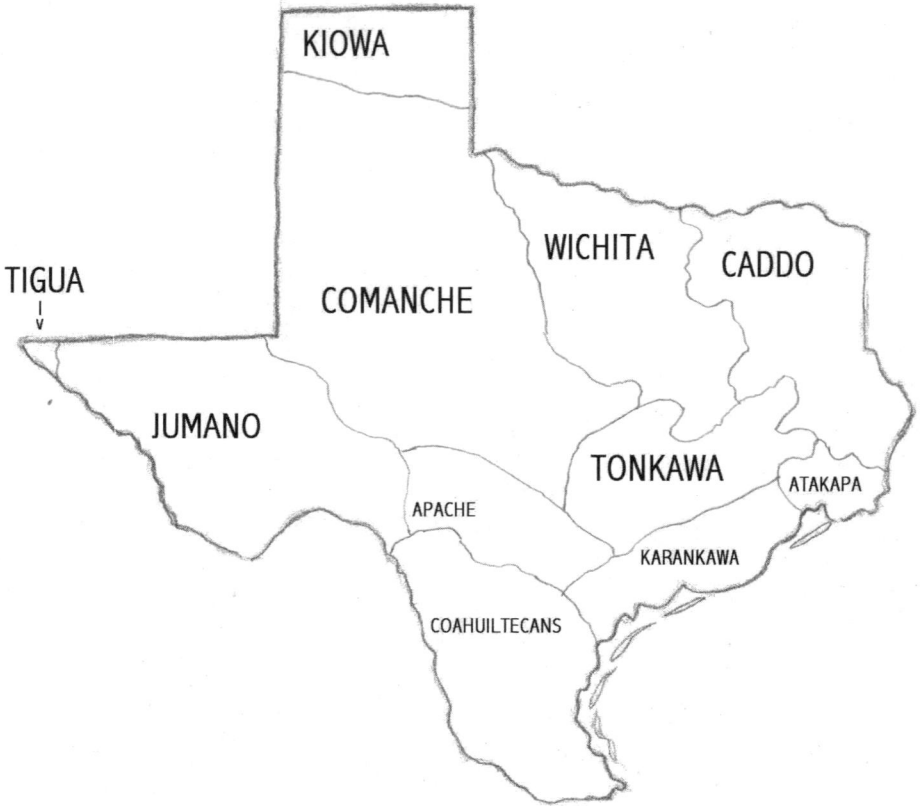

KIOWA

TIGUA

WICHITA

CADDO

COMANCHE

JUMANO

TONKAWA

ATAKAPA

APACHE

KARANKAWA

COAHUILTECANS

CONTENTS

CONTENTS

MAP OF COAHUITECAN REGION

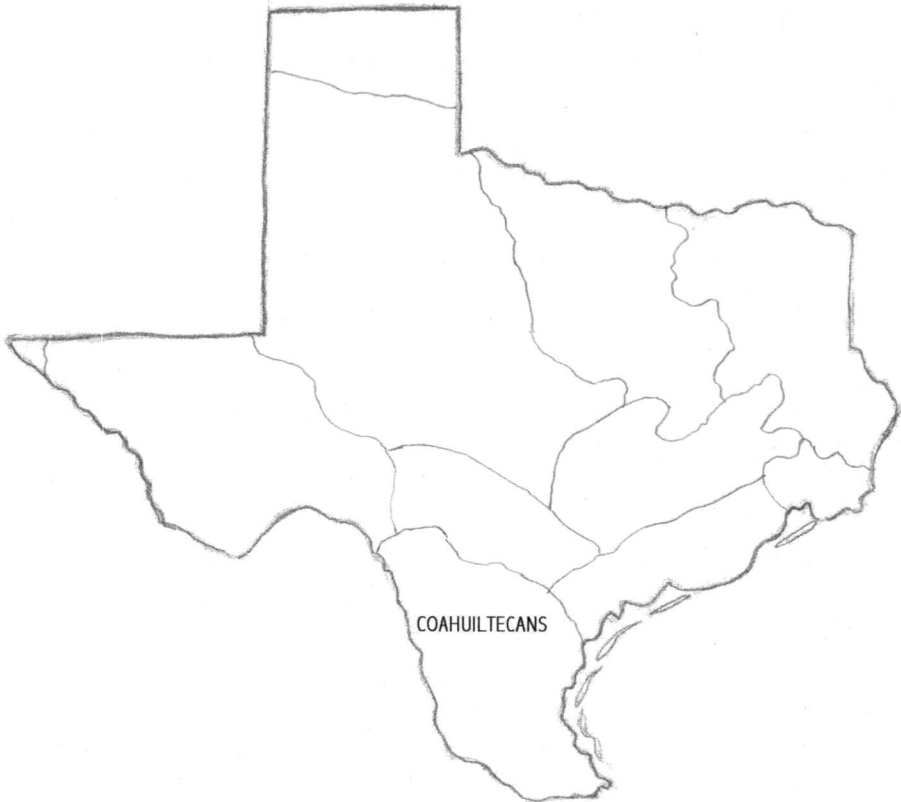

COAHUILTECANS

CHAPTER 1

COAHUILTECANS

LOCATION AND GOVERNMENT

The Coahuiltecans lived on the inland areas of the Texas Gulf Coastal Plain. This was the very dry rolling **plain** of south Texas. There was no land to farm, so these Natives were **primitive** hunters and gatherers. They lived in small, **nomadic**, related **bands.** They stayed in the area of the plain that belonged to their band. They were constantly moving from place to place looking for food, but they stayed within their area. The band was a small, independent part of a larger tribe. It was governed by a **chief** or headsman. Each band also had a **shaman**. He or she was the spiritual and medical person for the tribe.

HOW THEY LIVED

Life was very hard, probably the hardest of all the Native Texas tribes. The south Texas area they lived in is call Brush country because of its **vegetation.** The Coahuiltecans had to live off this land. This meant that they ate anything they could find. This included **prickly pears, mesquite beans**, snakes lizards, grubs, nuts, rabbit, deer, **javelina**, and anything else they could find. They hunted with bows made out of mesquite root with arrows made from hardwood and **flint**. Their tools were mostly made of flint, but they had an all-purpose stick tool made from wood.

DRESS

Because of the south Texas climate, the Coahuiltecans did not wear much clothing. They primarily wore **breechcloths** or **loincloths** which they liked to decorate with animal teeth, seeds, and anything else they could find. They wore fiber sandals. In bad weather they wore cloaks or robes made from animal skins. Women did most of the work. This is because the men were in constant search for food.

BELIEFS

The religious or spiritual beliefs of the Coahuiltecans were not very organized. Individual band members had their own personal beliefs. Shamans did hold religious like **ceremonies** for special events. An example of this would be becoming an adult. In this ceremony the child is tattooed by the shaman. Dreams were considered important. Marriages were arranged by the groom and the bride's parents. Deaths were taken very seriously, and **mourning** could last for as long as three months. Mourners sometimes starved to death because they did not search for food during this period and had to depend on others to eat. The **mitotes** were dances or festivals held by the band. They were usually to give thanks. They were often held to celebrate a victory, a good summer of food, or some other event for which they were thankful.

SUMMARY

The Coahuiltecan were a very **adaptable** tribal group. They managed to survive off the least productive land in Texas. They used whatever was available to them. They lived quite happily in this harsh **environment.**

MAP OF KARANKAWA REGION

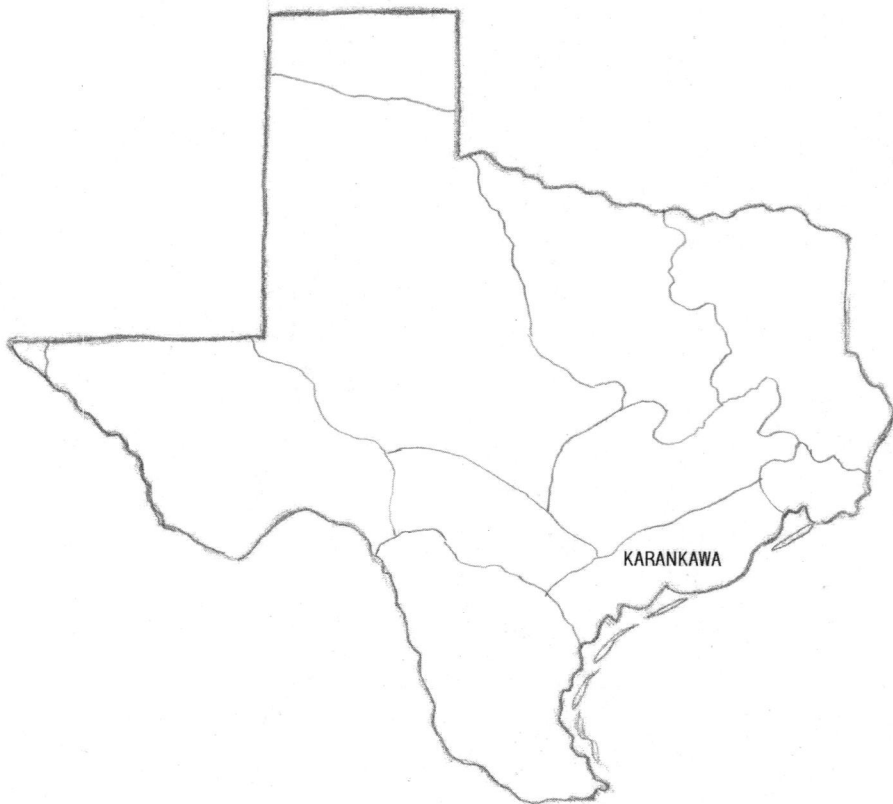

CHAPTER 2

KARANKAWA

LOCATION AND GOVERNMENT

For many centuries, if you traveled from west Galveston Bay to Corpus Christi Bay you would find Karankawa **bands** roaming over the area. Depending on the season, these nomadic groups lived on the **coastal prairie**, a narrow strip of land on the mainland of Texas, or on the islands near the

Texas coast. The Karankawa were made up of at least five groups or bands. Each of the bands was small, independent, and related to each other through their fathers. Each band had a **chief** that was always a man. Because it was difficult for a large **nomadic** group to feed itself, the Karankawa never developed into a **tribe.** When food was hard to find, the bands even broke up into small family units that were easier to feed. Smoke signals were used to bring the bands back together.

DRESS

The Karankawa were known for their unusual height. The men were at least 6 feet tall, very muscular, and well-built. They dressed in **breechcloths** made of animal skins. Karankawa women were considered attractive. Their dress was made of **Spanish moss** and **deerskin**. Both the men and women painted and tattooed their bodies. Young women had a small stripe from their forehead to their chin. These strips were expanded and became more detailed after marriage, and often included animals within the stripes. Tattooing was considered beautiful and often a **symbol** of an important event in their lives. The Karankawa often covered themselves in alligator lard and dirt to keep away mosquitoes.

HOW THEY LIVED

The Karankawa were very strong Natives who could withstand hunger, thirst, cold, and the **harshness** of the sun. Many animals lived in their area, but not enough of any one type to keep them feed. So, the Karankawa were nomadic **hunter-gatherers**. They were continually in search of food. Like most nomadic people, they traveled in a **pattern** and always returned to the same areas to find various types of food. They did not farm. In the fall, they would fish and eat underwater plant roots. From winter until the spring they ate shellfish, especially oysters, and then blackberries for a whole month. They hunted whatever animals they could find. These included deer, buffalo, **javelina, antelope,** bear, and small animals. When the food ran out, they moved on to another area.

TRANSPORTATION

Because the Karankawa spent so much time in the waters of the Texas gulf coast, they are famous for their dugout canoes. Even the explorer, **La Salle**, tried to trade for some of these canoes. They were made from tree trunks that were **hollowed** out. Each canoe was big enough to carry a whole family and their possessions. Poles were used to move the canoes through the water. They were very quiet, but only used for short trips because they were not very **sturdy.** Therefore, the Karankawa were expert swimmers.

HOMES

When not moving, the Karankawa lived in huts made from **willow** poles, woven mats, and animal skins. All of these materials were used to put together an **oval** shaped hut that was anywhere from 10 to 18 feet in **diameter**. Seven or eight people could live inside it, with a fire in the center for heat and cooking. Skins were used to sit on and to wrap up in for sleeping. These huts were easily taken apart and moved to their next camp by the women.

TOOLS

Karankawa **pottery** varied from jars, globe shaped vessels, and bowls, to possibly bottles. They also made baskets. Whether pottery or basket, they were coated inside and out with **asphaltum** for waterproofing. Food was cooked in the pottery by sinking the bottom into ashes or hot coals. Oysters were thrown into the fire or onto hot coals until they opened, then they were raked out of the fire and eaten. **Milling stones** were used to crush seeds and nuts.

WEAPONS

Though also used for fishing, the bow and arrow was the main weapon of the Karankawa. Their long bows were **proportioned** to the size of the man who owned it. The bows were made of **cedar** and the arrows of **cane** with three feathers and a stone point. The bow strings were made of deer **sinew**. The Karankawa also had **lances, clubs,** and **tomahawks**. Warfare was very common, and made trade very difficult. The Karankawa raided as far north as the Caddo Villages.

FAMILY, TRADITIONS, AND BELIEFS

The Karankawa were very fond of their children. Each child was given two names. One name was a nickname to be used in public and the other a secret name which the Kawakawa may have believed to be magical. Infants were attached to a cradle board and wrapped in a loop of skin which was worn by their mothers. As soon as they were able, children followed their parents. Girls worked with the women, and boys hunted and fished with their fathers. When children advance from childhood to adulthood a special **ceremony** was perform by the **shaman**. Marriage was arranged by the boy and the girl's parents. Gifts were given to the girl's parents. After arrangements were made the couple set up their own hut. For an agreed upon period of time, the husband gave his wife's father everything he hunted or fished. This was called **"bride service"**. During this time the bride's family feed them. At the end of this period the newly married couple joined the husband's band. From that point on, he and his in-laws could never talk, visit, or even look at each other. Kawakawa generally married for life. They were allowed to divorce if no children were born from the marriage.

Death was even more serious then marriage. Karakawas were buried in shallow graves except for the shaman who were **cremated**. Boys and men were mourned for a year. During this time their relatives wept for them three times each day. At the end of the year there was a **purification** ceremony for the relatives to end the mourning period. Only the old were not mourned. Their deaths were considered a good thing.

It is believed that the Karankawa had two main gods called **Pichini** and **Mel**. **Mitotes** were celebrated in their honor to give thanks for a good hunt or fishing trip. Mitotes were religious celebrations usually attended only by the men. There were other celebrations among the Karankawa. They enjoyed target shooting and knife throwing contests. They were very fond of wrestling matches, and played a ball game.

SUMMARY

As with the Coahuiltecans, the Texas gulf coast was a difficult place to live. The

Karankawa did their best to survive in that environment. These family groups used every available resource to make their lives the best they could, and passed these skills on to their children.

MAP OF ATAKAPA REGION

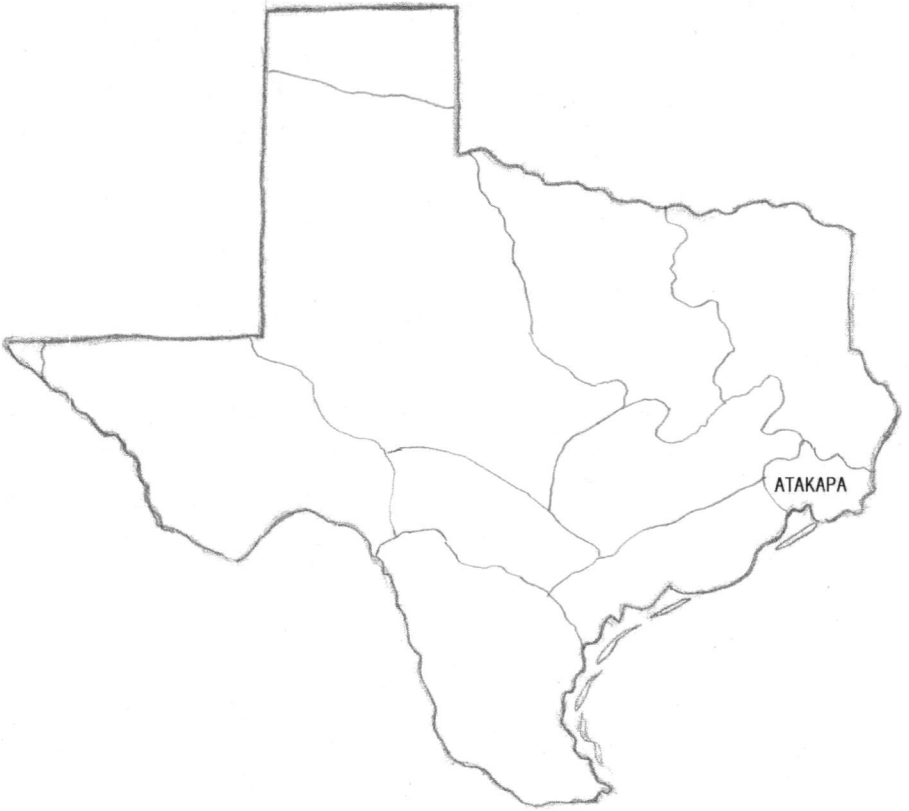

ATAKAPA

CHAPTER 3

ATAKAPA

LOCATION AND GOVERNMENT

Atakapa could be found in east Texas from Galveston Bay as far north as present day Huntsville to Jasper. There were four or five separate groups of Atakapa. They lived in various parts of this area. The group called Atakapa lived around the Sabine River from the coast to present day Jasper.

The Akokisas lived from Galveston Bay to about the area of present day Conroe. The Bidais lived in the northern area between the Trinity and Brazos rivers. These are three of the Atakapa groups we know something about because of their contact with the Europeans. They lived in small **bands**. They hunted separately. There was no overall leader or **chief** of the Atakapa. They seemed to respect age. They often broke up into even smaller family groups to hunt. Atakapa practiced slavery. Slaves often did what was considered women's work. This included carrying goods and getting water.

HOW THEY LIVED

Though each of the Atakapa groups had their own way of living, they were alike in many ways. All of the Atakapa groups fished, hunted and gathered. They searched for deer, bear, and buffalo throughout east Texas. They also **trapped** small animals. The women spent their time gathering wild roots and other plants. The Bidais did not go to the coast to fish, but the other Atakapa groups did. These Atakapa spent their summers along the **coast.** While there, they fished and collected shellfish and bird's eggs. The Atakapa traded for things they needed and could not hunt or gather for themselves. Women having babies were put in special huts by themselves. Older women of the tribe would take care of them until the baby was born. Newborns were strapped to a piece of **bark** bent to fit the baby's shape. The parents take the child's name. They are called father of or mother of the child from that point on. If the child should die they go back to their old names.

HOMES

The Atakapa homes were very much like the homes of the nomadic Natives of

Texas. They lived in small **lodges** that were made of tree branches covered with hides. **Shaman** huts were built on higher ground then the average member of the band. These huts were often built on piles of discarded shells.

DRESS AND WEAPONS

Atapaka dress was just like their surrounding neighbors. The men wore breechcloths, and the women wore skirts of Spanish moss and grasses. They also used tattoos. Atakapa also painted their bodies. The Atakapa used alligator oil to repel mosquitoes. Because of this oil, the people who met the Aakapa thought they smelled bad. The chief weapon of the Atakapa was the bow and arrow, but they also carried long **antler**-tipped spears.

BELIEFS

The Atakapa had beliefs that seemed to be very close to modern beliefs. They believed in a God. They also were taught not to do evil. They believed good people went up when they died, and the bad went down. They also believed in a great rain and flood. Shaman had a special place in society. They used **herbs**, as they preformed rituals and cures. They led all religious ceremonies.

SUMMARY

As you can see the Atakapa were much like the other Natives in their area. They clothes and homes were much like the other Natives. Hunting and gathering was the main way for them to get their food. Even though they had shaman, their religion was different and their beliefs were more like modern religion.

MAP OF CADDO REGION

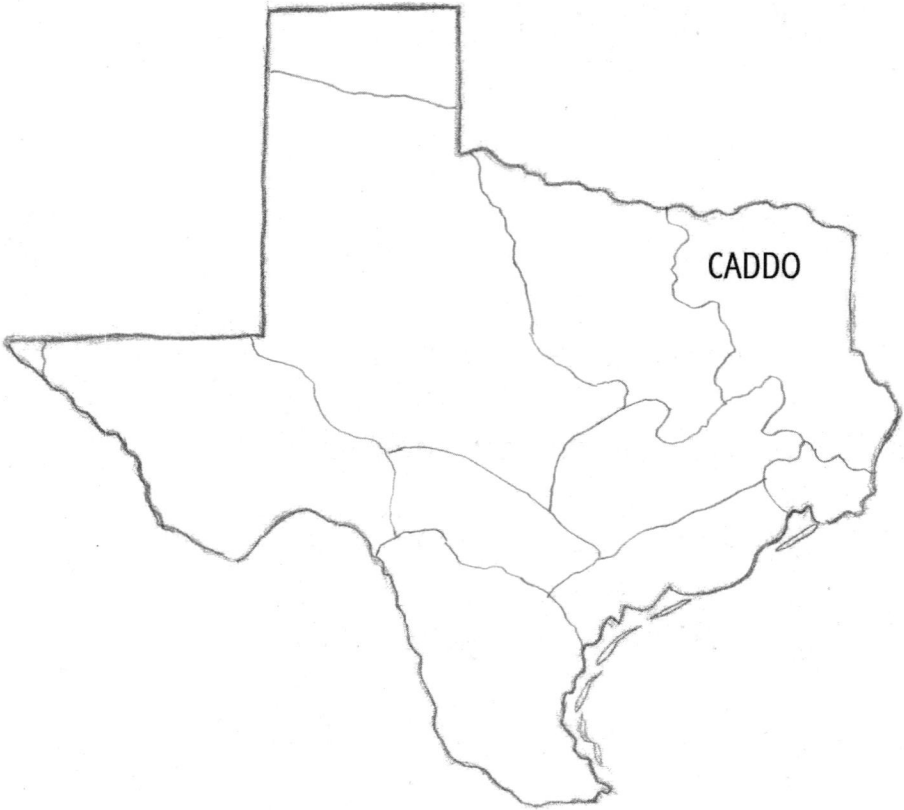

CADDO

CHAPTER 4

CADDO

LOCATION AND GOVERNMENT

The Caddo lived in the Piney Woods of East Texas. They settled around the rivers and their tributaries. You could find the Caddo along the Red, Angelina, Neches, Sabine, and Trinity Rivers. They also had a very complicated government. There was a chief called a caddi. This **chief** inherited his position and with the help of a council of wise men, kept order and solved problems within his tribe. Sometimes tribes would band together. Control would then go to a high chief called a **xinesí** (shenesi). These men were the top religious officials and were in charge of overseeing ceremonies and taking care of the **sacred fire**. They passed their position to their sons.

DRESS

Caddo men wore breechcloths made of deer skin. In colder weather they added buffalo robes, leggings, and moccasins.

Sometimes they wore their hair shoulder length, but more often they shaved or plucked all but the middle. The center hair went from forehead to neck in what we might call a **"Mohawk"**. They plucked out all of their facial hair.

The women wore **deerskin** skirts and buffalo robes. Their hair was worn long, parted in the middle, braided, and pulled together in the back. Both the men and the women wore necklaces, earrings, **pendants,** bracelets, and anklets. To make these they used shells, deer horns and hooves, and even rattlesnake rattles. They also painted and tattooed their bodies. They used thorns and charcoal to tattoo, and painted their bodies in streaks of various colors. Some of the tattoos were as simple as lines on a women chin, while others were more detailed designs of birds and animals.

HOMES

The Caddo homes, or **lodges**, looked a lot like beehives or haystacks. They were framed with logs or tree branches. Cane was used as roofing materials. The Caddo used grasses, straw and **thatch,** to cover the outside of their homes. Beds were made of reed matting which was laid over sticks and covered with buffalo skins. They took up one side of the lodge. Fires burned in the center of the lodge.

HOW THEY LIVED

The family was the most important unit in the tribe. Related families lived together in their lodges. When men married they moved into the lodge of their wife. The children belonged to their mother's clan. Women could divorce their husbands by simply throwing his belonging out of the lodge.

The Caddo were farmers. They lived on very good land for growing crops. The Caddo grew large fields of beans, squash, pumpkins, corn, and sunflowers. They had orchards of peaches, plums, figs and chestnut trees. The men cleared the fields, but the women planted and harvested. Women also harvested wild foods like fruit, berries, grapes, rice, and onions. The also gathered plants and herbs for healing. They were excellent **tanners.** They used hides to make blankets, clothing, rope, and lashing materials.   The men and boys protected, hunted and fished to add to the food supply. They built lodges, made tools, and moccasins.   They were excellent **potters**. They made coiled clay containers for holding food. The Caddo made bottles, jars, bowls, cups, and other vessels. Figurines were made and used in ceremonies.   Others were made for children's toys. They also made beads and pipes. Some of the potter painted their work with designs. The men also turned animal bones into tools, hairpins, and combs. They were also good traders.

They traded lances, shields, pottery, baskets, mats, and drums.

BELIEFS

The Caddo believed in one god or **Great Spirit** who created the world. They also believed in a devil. There were also lesser spirits. These were made up of spirits of **ancestors**, people, animals, storms, clouds, trees, and rocks. There was a Corn Goddess, **Mother Earth,** and the Sacred Fire God. These were important because they needed corn to eat, which came from the earth, and was cooked over fire.

The Caddo were mound builders. They built hills of cane and grass. At the top of these hills they built their temples, priests' homes, and homes for important families. These mounds were where the Caddo held the religious ceremonies and buried their leaders. The xinesí was the top religious official. They believed they descended from the moon. He kept the sacred fire burning.

SUMMARY

The Caddo were great farmers of the Piney Woods of East Texas. They created pottery, baskets, mats, and other goods they could trade. They lived in villages. Government was controlled by chiefs who were also their religious leaders. Caddo believed in a creator, and tried to live a good life in land that had plenty to offer.

MAP OF WICHITA REGION

WICHITA

CHAPTER 5

WICHITA

LOCATION AND GOVERNMENT

The Wichita were found near the eastern edges of the **Great Plains**. They were located west-northwest of the Caddo, and shared many things in common with them. They had **chiefs** that led their groups. Chiefs were assisted by sub chiefs. When there were problems, the adult men of the tribe were asked for their advice. Warriors smoked the **peace pipe** to show they were serious about reaching a good decision. When not in use, this special pipe was kept by the group's chief. The **Shaman** was religious leaders for the tribe.

HOMES

The homes of the Wichita were beehive shaped. They were made of branches and **thatch** much like the Caddo. They held an **extended family** with 10 to 15 **pallets** on one side. If the family got too big for the home, one or two of the individual families would build a new house nearby.

The Wichita also built an **arbor** next to their

house. This was done with four poles and a

roof. The purpose of the arbor was to give

the women a shady place to do their work.

DRESS

The Wichita women were the most

dressed of all the Natives. They wore

clothes made of tanned hides that covered

them from their chins to their ankles. They

also wore necklaces made of **elk** teeth. Men

wore shirts and breechcloths with **leggings**.

Both the women and men wore earrings,

necklaces, and other jewelry. They also both used tattoos. They were so tattooed around their eyes that they looked like they had raccoon eyes. They were even called raccoon eyes because of this custom.

HOW THEY LIVED

The Wichita were farmers, but since they lived so close to the Great Plains they also hunted buffalo. As farmers, the Wichita planted large fields of corn, beans, and squash. They also planted pumpkins, watermelon, **muskmelon,** and plum trees. Field work was traditionally done by the women. There was a yearly buffalo hunt. Each year, they would move west on to the plains and hunt buffalo. After the hunt they moved back to their farms.

Wichita also traded. They made long bows from **Bois d'Arc** (bwa dark) wood, which means bow wood. This was a very hard but flexible yellow wood from **Osage-orange** tree. This tree was very common in the area in which the Wichita lived. It has been said that bows made of this wood earned a very good price. Besides the bow, they traded elk teeth necklaces, tobacco, corn, and beans. They traded for Comanche horses, buffalo hide, and buffalo meat. They took some of the horses and traded them for French guns and **ammunition** and Caddo pottery.

The Wichita lines descended through their mothers. When a man married he moved into his wife's family home. The man then provided food for his in-laws as well as himself and his wife.

BELIEFS

The Wichita looked to the sky for their gods. Their general beliefs were not much different then modern beliefs. They believed in a chief God, a creator named Man-Never-Known-On-Earth. They believed he created the universe and the first man and woman. They also believed in **Mother Earth**. She allowed the crops to grow. Shaman led ceremonies and many had to do with food. There were many ceremonies, prayers, and gathering during the corn growing season. The rest of their gods came from the sky and stars. These included the Sun, Morning Star, North Star, South Star, Moon, Ghost Star, and many others. They believed in the **afterlife.** Wichita believe that good people were reward and bad people punished in the afterlife. This led the Wichita to be well behaved, obedient, and polite.

SUMMARY

The Wichita were very similar to their neighbors the Caddo. They lived in beehive shaped homes, tattooed their bodies, and traded. They also had a yearly hunt for buffalo and moved west for a while once a year to hunt. They descended through their mother's family. Wichita believed in a creator and in an afterlife with reward and punishment.

MAP OF APACHE REGION

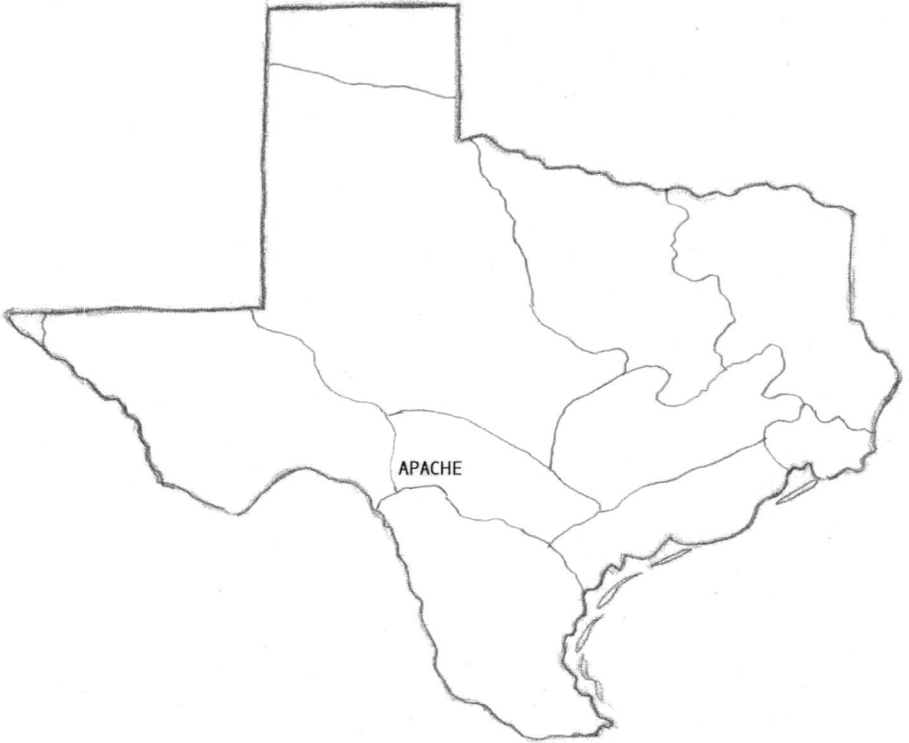

APACHE

CHAPTER 6

APACHE

LOCATION

The Apaches were actually several

groups of Natives that probably moved

down to the southern plains of the United

States from Canada. The word Apache is a

pueblo word which means enemy. Two of

the Apache groups could be found in Texas,

the **Lipan** and **Mescalero.** The Lipan lived

northwest of present day San Antonio around the upper Colorado, Brazos, and Red rivers. The Mescalero lived around Pecos and Rio Grande.

DRESS

Unlike many of the other Texas Natives, the Apache did not tattoo themselves, but they did use paint, especially around their eyes. They pierced their ears, and wore copper and shell jewelry. Buffalo and deer provided the materials for all of their clothing. During warm weather, the men dressed in

breechcloth and the women in **deerskin** skirts. When the weather was cold, both men and women wore leggings, moccasins, shirts, and **ponchos**. The Apache were famous for their moccasin-boots with turned-up toes. In the very cold weather, they wrapped themselves in blankets made of buffalo hide. The more contact the Apaches had with the Europeans, the more beads and metal they used on their clothing. The women had long hair which they kept in a braid at their back. Apache men cut the hair on the left side level with the top of their ear. They let the right side grow long,

but tied it up to shoulder length.

HOW THEY LIVED

The Apache were hunter-gathers. The

main source of food for the Apache was the

buffalo.   They also hunted deer, **antelope**,

javelina, rats, wild turkeys, and wild cattle.

Buffalo hunting was done in groups. A

leader was elected to run the hunt and sub

leaders helped him. After finding a herd,

near a watering area, they would surround it.

Bows and arrows were used to shoot the

animals and spears were thrown. After European contact, they learned to use guns. They continued to use the **surround** method of hunting even after they had horses. Buffalos were immediately opened and eaten. Left over meat was made into jerky which is dried or smoked meat.

Though they never really lived by farming, Apache women did sometimes raise gardens. They usually grew *maize,* beans, squash, and pumpkins. If they were not grown, the Apaches would trade for these vegetables. One wild plant that was a favorite of the Lipan was the **agave.** They used the fibers to make baskets and sandals, and the **bulbs** for food.

HOMES

The Apaches of the plains lived in tepees made of light poles and buffalo hides. The poles were usually **sotol** stalks that were placed in a circle, tied at the top, and covered with the hides. These homes varied in size. They could be big enough for 12 people or small enough for 3 or 4. The entry hole was small, and could easily be covered with hides. Beds were made of piles of grass or cedar twigs covered with buffalo hides fur side up. Tepees were easy to move. Some of the Apaches lived in more sturdy homes called **lodges.**

GOVERNMENT

Unlike many of the Texas Natives, the Apache family structure was dependent on their mother. The groom's parents had to arrange the marriage with the bride's parents. It was the wife's **band** that the newlyweds joined. The husband had to listen to and greatly respect his in-laws. The wife's brother was the person who looked out for her and her children. They lived in these family bands that were loosely organized under a **chief.** A chief proved himself by age, skill, and wisdom. Some families were expected to produce chiefs.

WEAPONS AND WAR

Most trusted and used weapon of the Apache was the bow and arrow. Apache bows were usually 4 feet long and made of **seasoned** mountain **mulberry.** Bowstrings were made of deer or buffalo **sinew.** The arrows, which were always kept dry, were made of hardwood with three feathers and tipped first with **flint** and later on with an

iron point. It was said an Apache could shoot a dozen arrows in the time it took to load a musket. They also had lances made of steel blades attached to wooden handles. Apaches carried oval shields made of bison hides. They were 3 feet by 2 feet, and nothing could go through unless it was hit straight and in center.

Apache boys began training for war at a very early age. Running, wrestling, and pretend battles were used to test their strength and **stamina**. They were taught methods of war and how to raid. Apaches were feared throughout Texas. They scalped those they killed and tortured their captives. The Apache had a reputation as **fierce** warriors.

TRANSPORTATION

At first the Apache traveled and hunted on foot. Hunting on foot was very dangerous. The Apache could not out run the buffalo. When traveling, their goods were pulled or carried by shaggy dogs. After contact with the Spanish, the Apaches adopted the horse. Horses made hunting much easier, but also improved transporting their goods.

BELIEFS

Apaches believed in gods. They believed the gods caused things like lightening and thunder. They believed witches caused bad things to happen, and they were afraid of ghosts. Seeing ghosts would bring about troubles, even death, so they were careful in burying their dead. They never spoke the dead person's name and moved away from the grave.

A shaman had **supernatural** powers. So, anyone could be a shaman as long as they possessed these special powers. **Shaman** could pass on their powers to another. If the powers were misused, even after they were passed on, the original owner could still be punished. So, they usually waited until they were old to pass them to another.

SUMMARY

The Apache moved from Canada to the plains of Texas. They changed from hunter-gatherers, who sometimes farmed, to great hunters. As hunters, they took over the buffalo hide trade on the Texas plains. Though very **superstitious** and afraid of ghosts, even their name brought fear to

many people in their area.

MAP OF TONKAWA REGION

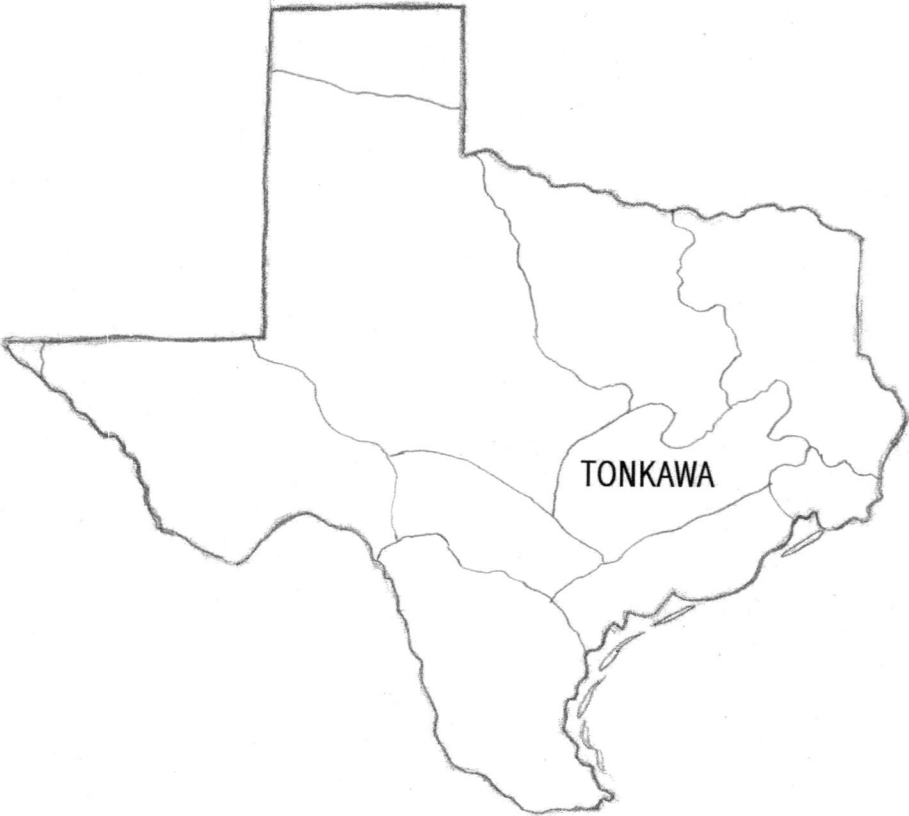

TONKAWA

CHAPTER 7

TONKAWA

LOCATION

The Tonkawa's original homeland was the hill country of central Texas. As their enemies, the Comanche and Apache, pushed them further away from the buffalo, they ended up on the edges of the Edwards **plateau** and the coastal plains. Luckily, this area was rich in animals, fish, nuts, berries and roots. The area also had many fresh springs which supplied their water.

GOVERNMENT

Even though they lived in small **nomadic bands**, all Tonkawa were members of a larger **clan.** Clan members were related through their mothers. Children, both boys and girls, were part of their mother's clan. Each clan had a **chief,** but there was also an overall Tonkawa chief. Clans also had a special guardian. They were usually an animal or some sort of spirit like modern day team mascots. All

Tonkawa traced their beginnings back to a great wolf.

HOMES

The Tonkawa built homes much like the other Texas nomadic Natives. Two things were different about the Tonkawa homes though. They used poles made from available tree branches and covered them with brush and grasses. Their homes were **cone** shaped.

DRESS

Tonkawa tattooed and painted their bodies. Tattoos were very important. They helped to tell what band a Tonkawa belonged to because every band had different tattoos. Tattoos were owned by their wearer. No one could use their tattoos without permission. Tonkawa men wore very long **breechcloths**. They also wore moccasins and leggings. Men wore their hair long, parted in the middle, and often braided. The women wore short skirts. During winter they both added buffalo robes. Earring and necklaces of bone and shell were also worn.

HOW THEY LIVED

The Tonkawa believed that they began with a wolf. Wolves are hunter. So, the Tonkawa were **hunter-gatherers.** The buffalo was the source of everything they needed. Every part of the animal was used. The Apache made hunting the buffalo very difficult for the Tonkawa. The Tonkawa also hunted smaller animals like deer. It was lucky that they lived in an area that also had small animals, rivers for fish, nuts, roots, and berries. Even rattlesnake was considered a very special treat.

The Tonkawa traded for other things they needed.   They would use sign language to talk to other people. They traded with the Caddo for pottery. They did not make their own. Tonkawa also traded for horses. The horse was very important for hunting buffalo. They would steal horses when they couldn't trade for them.

WEAPONS AND WARFARE

The bow and arrow was the best and most favored weapon of the Tonkawa.

Arrows had stone points until they got metal from the Europeans. Tonkawa believed that their arrow points were poisoned by putting the liquid from the **mistletoe** leaf on them. Even when they got guns, they would pour this liquid down the gun barrels. Lances were also used during war and sometimes for hunting. When at war, they carried bison hide shields and wore jackets and helmets made of tough hide.

BELIEFS

We know that the Tonkawa had **shaman**, but we don't know too much about what they did. Death was a very complicated ceremony. The hair was cut from a person who died. His face painted yellow, and body wrapped. He was also buried with many of his things. Anything that he had with him when he died was destroyed. His band **mourned** for three days. His family mourned for a longer time. When the mourning period was over the chief talked to the band, and the person's name was never said or used again. They did not want to call the spirit back to this world. Probably the most holy and serious of their ceremonies was the wolf dance. It honored their beginnings with the great wolf.

SUMMARY

The Tonkawa had many things in common with the other Texas Natives like hunting buffalo and wearing tattoos and paint. Unlike the other Natives they believed that they owed their existence to a great wolf. They also owned their tattoo designs which linked them to their band. They lived in cone shaped huts and traded for things they could not get on their own. This made them very friendly toward the

Spanish and the Anglo settlers that came

later to Texas.

MAP OF KIOWA REGION

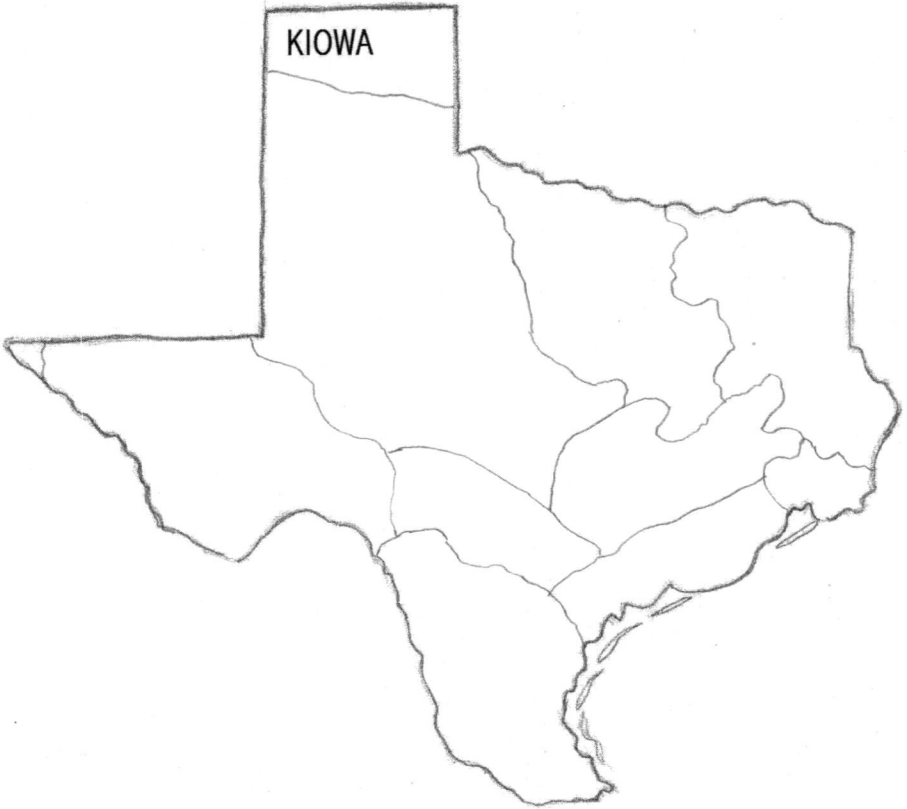

CHAPTER 8

KIOWA

LOCATION AND GOVERNMENT

The Kiowa could be found in the Texas Panhandle. They started out in Palo Duro Canyon but were pushed farther south by other tribes and ended up in Comanche territory. At first this caused fighting, but as time went on the Comanche and Kiowa became **allies.** The basic unit of the Kiowa was a group of brothers. They with their wives and relatives form an **extended family.** These units grouped themselves into bands. Only men held the band's leadership positions. Sons were important, and the favorite son most of all. Fathers would do everything in their power to improve their son's place in **society**. They would give feast in their honor and would even buy powerful names from warriors who were too old to go into battle. There was only two ways for a Kiowa to really gain power on his own, the buffalo hide trade and as a warrior.

DRESS

Kiowa men wore shirts, **breechcloths** and **moccasins** all made of deer hide. The women wore dresses and tall moccasins of **deerskin**. In cold weather both protected themselves with buffalo robes. The Kiowa loved metal. They decorated their clothes and horses with silver and other metals. Men wore their hair long. In early times, they often cut the right side short to show off their earrings. Women had long hair that they parted in the center and braided.

HOMES

The Kiowa were nomadic hunter-gathers. Their home had to be moveable. They lived in tepees. Their homes were made starting with four poles, and then they added twenty more poles. These poles were covered with **tanned** buffalo hides that were sewn together. The entrance to these tepees was a circle opening that faced east and was raised off the ground.

HOW THEY LIVED

Because the Kiowa were nomadic and followed the herds, the horse became very important to them. They did not farm. They did add to their buffalo **diet** in two ways. The women gathered fruits, berries, roots, and nuts. The men also hunted smaller animals like deer and antelope. The Kiowa did not eat bear, birds, or fish. They had no pottery or baskets.

The Kiowa men divided themselves into six ranked groups. The groups were not determined by band, but by **character**. All boys started out in Rabbits. Some stay Rabbits for life, and that was not seen as a bad thing. Only ten men belonged to the highest of the groups, the Real Dogs.

Personal characteristics like bravery, generosity and wisdom moved a man into a higher group. Only the best and bravest became Real Dogs. They wore red painted deerskin sashes to show who they were and their **rank.**

Kiowa weapons were the lance and the bow and arrow. Kiowa **quivers** were only made of panther skin or Mexican leather but never hide. They hunted using the **surround method**. The top men policed the hunt to make sure everything went well. Men took turns shooting at the buffalo. Sometimes, they drove the herd to the edge of a cliff so the animals would tumble off and die. The women tanned the hides and they were very good at tanning. One of the important uses for the buffalo hide was the Kiowa **buffalo story hide**. Not only was it a written record of major events in the Kiowa history, but it was also a beautiful work of art. The hide was decorated with artists' pictures of all the events of each year.

BELIEFS

The Sun Boy was the most important of the Kiowa gods. He was believed to be the creator of the Kiowa people. He gave

them the ten sacred **medicine bundles.**
These bundles were held by different
families. This was a very important job. The
bundle keepers were important people and
were often asked to help solve problems.
The Sun Dance was their most holy
ceremony. It took place in late spring or
early summer, usually sometime in June. It
bought all of the Kiowa together. The
purpose of the ceremony was to ask for good
hunting, good health, and victory at war. It
was a very happy time for the Kiowa.

SUMMARY

The Kiowa were hunter-gatherers of the Texas Panhandle. They lived in bands, but the men divided themselves into six ranked groups from Rabbits to Real Dogs. Sons were very important to their families. Their lives totally centered on the buffalo. They did not farm. They were allies with the Comanche. They worshiped many gods, but most important was the Sun god.

MAP OF COMANCHE REGION

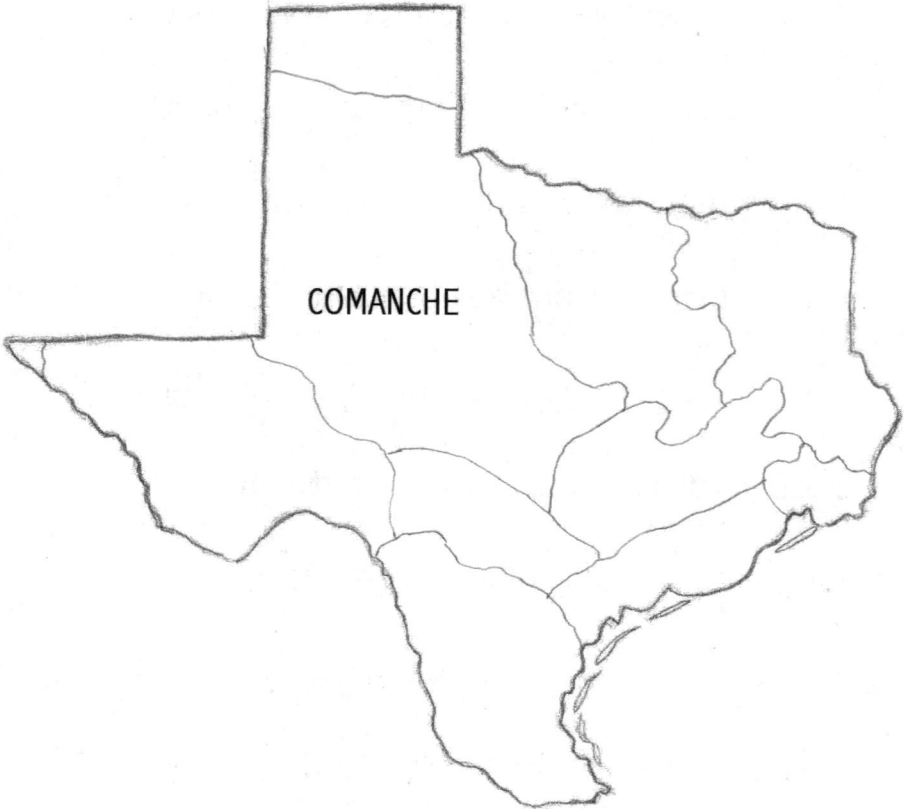

COMANCHE

CHAPTER 9

COMANCHE

LOCATION AND GOVERNMENT

The Comanche lived on the Great

Plains of west Texas. Their land, called the

Comanchería, was the largest area of all the

Texas Natives. They controlled the area

from the **cross timbers** of central Texas to

the staked plains of northwest Texas. They

shared part of this land with their **allies**, the

Kiowa, but no one else was welcome on their land.

We call the Comanche a **tribe,** but they really were not a tribe. They never gathered all together at one time for any reason. Comanche lived in **bands** that were connected through blood relations or common interest. There were up to twelve bands. Some bands were more important than others. The band **chiefs** were chosen by members of the band. They had to keep the people happy and do a good, fair job, or they would be replaced. A war chief was chosen by warriors, and usually only for one

campaign.

HOMES

The Comanche were nomadic hunter-gatherers who traveled by horse. Their homes had to be moveable. They lived in buffalo hide tepees. They used 12 to 14 feet poles that were covered with tanned buffalo hides. They even decorated their homes with paint and beads. The entrance was covered with a bearskin. The Comanche had a flap at the top where the poles were strapped together which allowed the smoke from their fire to escape. They use skins for seats and beds.

DRESS

Unlike so many of the Texas Natives, Comanche did not tattoo their bodies. They dressed in hides. The men wore **breechcloths** and **moccasins** in the warm weather. When it got cold they add buffalo robes, **leggings**, and hide boots.   The men spent a great deal of time on their hair. They let it grow as long as possible, parted it in the center, and made two braids which they wrapped with cloth or fur. The men also wore many earrings. The women wore **buckskin** skirts and blouses. They decorated the blouses with paint and beads. They added robes and more clothing when it got colder. The women did not worry about their hair. They just cut it, parted it in the center, and let it hang. Both the men and women painted the parts in their hair.

HOW THEY LIVED

The horse was the most important possession of the Comanche Natives. They had more horses than any other tribe. They controlled the land of the **wild mustangs**. A

Comanche learned to ride at a very early age. They were excellent horsemen.

Boys were important to the Comanche. They were tied on their first horse when one or two years old. This way they learned to ride quickly. They learned how to shoot with a bow and arrow and how to kill and prepare a buffalo. After the boy's first kill his band celebrated the **eagle dance** in his honor. He was given clothing and weapons decorated with eagle feathers for good luck.

Food, clothing, shelter, and tools were all made from the buffalo. The Comanche followed the herd. They always tried to

camp near running water. The biggest and
best hunts were in summer and fall. At this
time the buffalo was fat and their coats the
best. Everyone worked together during the
hunt. They all had a part to play and they
did it well. Buffalo was not the only animal
hunted. The Comanche also hunted **elk**,
black bear for its oil, antelope and deer.
The Comanche did not farm. They collected
wild plants to balance their diet. Plums,
grapes, currants, juniper berries, mulberries,
persimmon, prickly pears, pecans, acorns,
roots, and **tubers** were all collected by the
Comanche.

WEAPONS AND WARFARE

The main weapon of the Comanche was the bow and arrow. They preferred bows made of **Bois d'Arc** (bwa dark), but used **hickory** when it was not available. Their bows were only about three feet long because they were easier to shoot from their horses. Their arrows were made of **dogwood** and iron tipped. They also carried bison hide shields. Their shields were decorated to show they were good hunters, warriors, and **raiders**. Feathers were attached to the shield to throw off their enemies aim.

The Comanche were **fierce** warriors. They earned awards from their band for bravery and other acts of war. There was great **rivalry** among the Texas Natives. They fought over buffalo, horses, and land. This naturally led to wars between the Natives and with the settlers when they arrived in Texas.

BELIEFS

Religion or belief was very individual for the Comanche. Each individual Comanche searched for his own **"medicine"** when he was ready. He went on a **vision**

quest. He took only four things with him, a buffalo robe, a pipe, tobacco, and a way to light the pipe. He was prepared by the **shaman** and then set out alone on his quest. During the vision the Comanche was given his special "medicine" to do good. If he used the power in a bad way, it turned from good to evil. Women got their power through their husbands.

SUMMARY

The Comanche were the horsemen of the Native Texans. They lived in bands that were made up of related families. All of their possessions were made from the buffalo. They were nomadic because they had to follow the herds. They fought to protect their lands in order to survive. The Comanche were feared throughout Texas because they were fierce warriors.

MAP OF JUMANO REGION

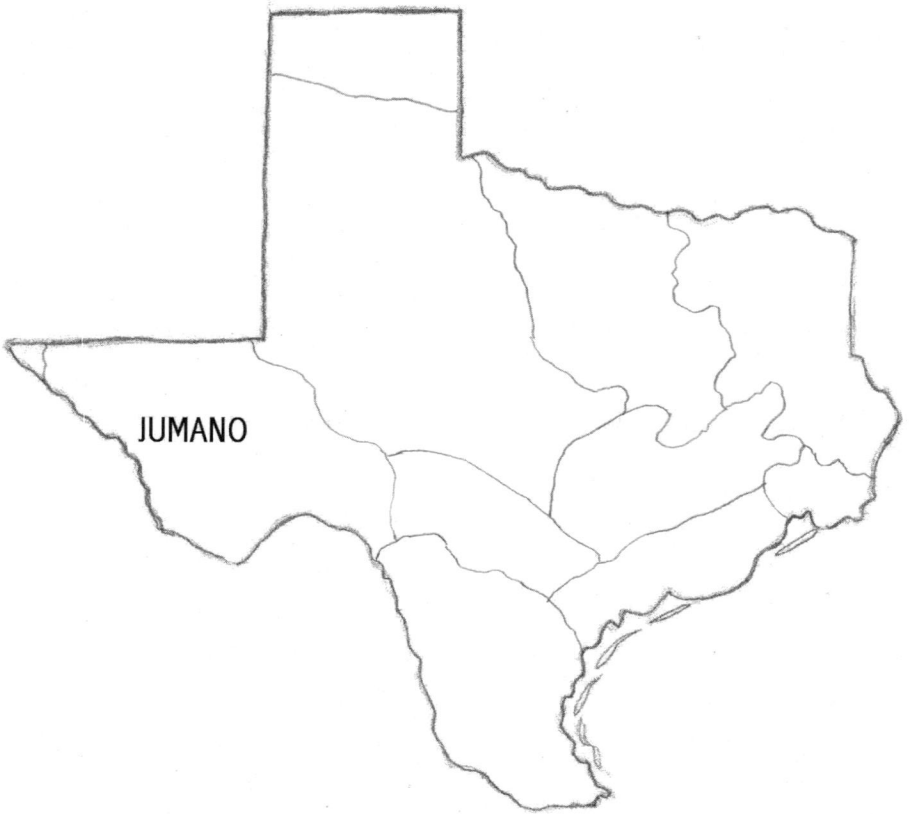

JUMANO

CHAPTER 10

JUMANO

LOCATION AND ORANIZATION

There were actually at least two groups

of Jumano Natives. The Jumanos that

farmed for a living, stayed in one place. The

other groups were **hunter-gatherers** who

traded across Texas. Those who farmed

lived in large towns along the Rio Grande

and Concho Rivers. These villages went as

far west as present-day El Paso. Each of these villages was run by a **chief.** The chief settled problems that came up among the villagers. These Natives were called **Pueblo Jumanos** because they lived in homes called pueblos.

The **nomadic** groups, called **Plains Jumanos**, hunted buffalo between the Rio Grande and the Pecos River. We do not know exactly how these nomadic groups were governed. So, the Jumanos lived in most of the area of Texas west of the Pecos River.

DRESS

Like so many of the other Texas Natives, the Jumanos tattooed and painted their bodies. The women wore their hair long. Men cut their hair short to about the middle of their scalp. They used paint to curl what was left into what looked like a cap or bun, but left a lock of hair in the middle. They tied feathers to this lock of hair. The men wore buffalo hides. The women wore **deerskin** skirts and **ponchos** sometimes adding buffalo hide cloaks.

HOMES

The farming Jumanos, lived in flat roofed houses made of adobe or dried mud called **pueblos.** These were very strong houses. The Natives could even stand on their flat roofs. The homes were partly underground. They were cool and easy to repair. Plains Jumanos lived in the usual home of a nomadic Native. Their homes were made of sticks and hides and were easy to pick up and move.

HOW THEY LIVED

In the Jumano farming villages they grew corn, beans, squash, **gourds**, and cotton. These were all grown using rain. The Jumanos did not bring water to their crops. Women also gathered **mesquite pods and beans** to make a type of flour. They also cooked **agave bulbs**. They used earth ovens. They also harvested **prickly pears** and the fruit of other cacti. They gathered salt from **lagoons** and river **marshes**. This was not only used by the Jumanos, but they also traded salt to other Native groups.

Both groups of Jumano lived in the driest area of Texas. They often had to deal with **droughts.** The farming groups built **granaries** to store their food during these times. Survival was still difficult, so men hunted deer, **fowl,** and buffalo. They also fished. Even the farming Jumanos traded for thing they needed. The Jumanos were part of a large trade **network** that existed long before the Europeans arrived. The Jumanos used bows and arrows. They had bottle gourds, gourds for storage, and for cooking. They made utensils from buffalo and deer. They had simple brown **pottery.**

BELIEFS

We do not know too much about the Jumanos belief system. We do know that they had **ceremonies**. Music was important to them. They would sing, clap in time, and dance in some of the ceremonies.

SUMMARY

We do not know very much about the Jumanos. What we do know comes from their contact with the Europeans. The Jumanos adapted very well to the driest region of Texas. Some of the Jumano lived near the rivers and farmed, while other groups were nomadic hunter-gatherers. They were an important part of a great Native trade network that crossed Texas.

MAP OF TIGUAS REGION

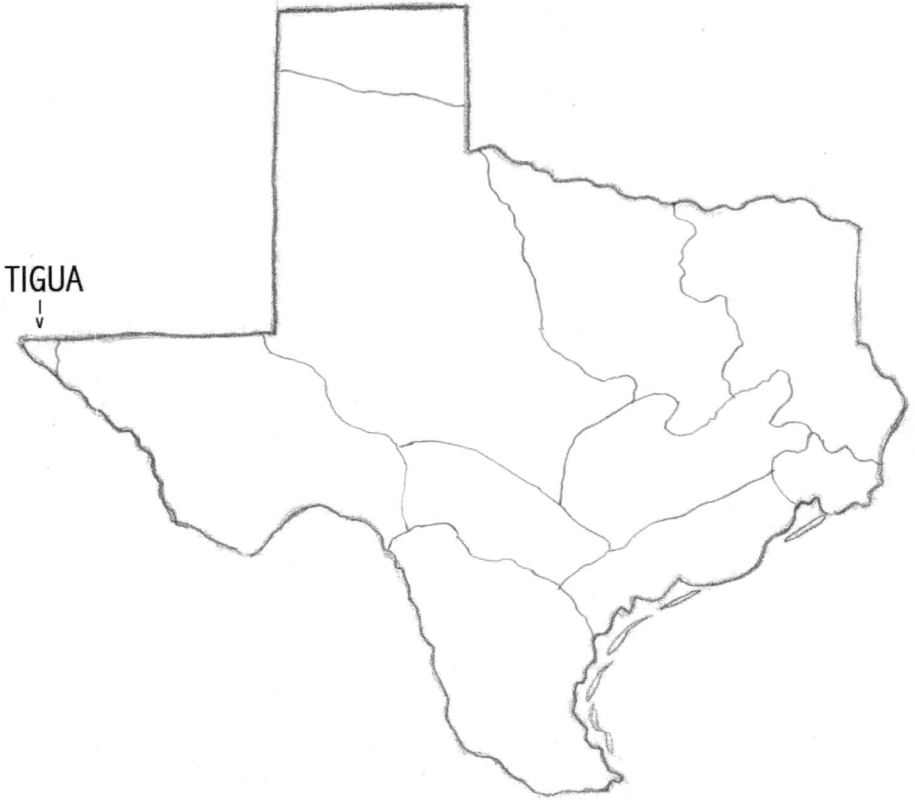

TIGUA

CHAPTER 11

TIGUAS

LOCATION AND GOVERNMENT

The Tiguas moved into Texas with the Spanish and settled in the area we know as El Paso in far west Texas. The Tiguas were governed by a **chief.** He was also their **medicine man.** He did not govern alone. Under the chief there were three **ranks.** Directly under the chief was the governor.

He was like an assistant chief. Next in line came the war chief. The final level of government was the captain. The Tiguas had four captains.

HOMES

The Tiguas are called Pueblo Natives because of their homes. They built **traditional pueblo** homes when they moved to Texas. These pueblos were like modern apartment buildings. They had three or more stories, and were divided into small apartments. Hundreds of related families could live in these buildings. It was important to the Tiguas culture to live near family. The Tiguas built their pueblos around a **plaza** where people could walk and meet each other. As time went on, their pueblos crumbled and the Tiguas began living in small huts made of branches and mud called **jacale.**

HOW THEY LIVED

The Tiguas were farmers. They grew corn. The men cleared the fields and dug **ditches** to bring water from the Rio Grande to the fields. They had no problems with **drought**. Tigua men also hunted wild game to add to their food supply and they raised sheep. The women planted the fields with corn, beans, melons, and squash. Women also grew cotton which they used to make clothes along with the wool from their sheep. Children worked with their mothers in the fields. The women and girls also gathered wild foods to add to their **diet.** The Tiguas also made **pottery.**

BELIEFS

Tigua's beliefs said that they came to this world from underground. The legend says a **badger** dug a hole. From this hole, the Tigua reached up and grabbed a spruce tree. They used the spruce tree to pull themselves out. When they met the Spanish, they took on many **Christian** beliefs. They mixed these Christian ideas with their own. Their celebrations revolved around their crops and the hunt. They celebrated all stages of the corn crop. The biggest celebration was at harvest time. They also had **rituals** for their hunts. They showed Christian beliefs through their devotion to St. Anthony. The Tigua believed he protect them and their homes. They have a big celebration to honor him on June 13th every year.

SUMMARY

The Tiguas were a small group of Natives that came from the west into Texas with the Spanish. They were farmers. They brought water from the Rio Grande to their fields. They never worried about drought. They hunted and gathered to add to their food supply. They were a spiritual group. They blended their beliefs with the Christian beliefs taught by the Spanish.

BIBLIOGRAPHY

Cabeza de Vaca, Alar Nuñez. Trans.

Cyclone Covey, ed. *The Journey and*

Ordeal of Cabeza De Vaca: His

Account of the Disastrous First

European Exploration of the American

Southwest. Mineola: Dover

Publications, Inc.,2003.

Cantrell, Gregg. *Stephen F. Austin:*

Empresario of Texas. New Haven:

Yale University Press, 1999.

Fehrenbach, T. R. *Lone Star: A History of*

Texas and the Texans. New York:

Da Capo Press, 2000.

Jurney, David H. "The Original Distribution
Of Bois D'Arc." *Caddoan Arcaeology
Newsletter* July 1994. Southern
Methodist University Anthropology,
23 June 2005 <http://www.smu.edu/
anthro/collections/boisdarc.html>.

La Vere, David. *The Texas Indians.* College
Station: Texas A&M University Press,
2004.

Newcomb, W. W., Jr. *The Indians of Texas:
From Prehistoric To Modern Times.*
Austin: University of Texas Press,
1961.

Smallwood, James M. *The Indian Texans.* College Station: Texas A&M University Press, 2004.

Solis, Jose de. *The Solis Diary of 1767.* Trans. Rev. Peter P.Forrestal. Texas Catholic Historical Society 1931 19 June 2005 <http://www.tamu.edu/cbn/ dewitt/alarco nex5.htm >.

Smithwick, Noah. *The Evolution of a State Or Recollections of Old Texas Days.* Austin: University of Texas Press, 1983.

Weddle, Robert S. *The Wreck of the Belle,*

The Ruin of La Salle. College Station:

Texas A&M University Press, 2001.

GLOSSARY

Adaptable adj. able to adjust to something new

Afterlife n. life after death

Agave n. a plant found in American deserts

Allies n. friends

Ammunition n. bullets and other things used in battle

Ancestor n. a person from whom one descends

Antelope n. an animal with hoofs and horns related to deer

Antler n. a solid horn of animal usually of the deer family

Arbor n. a shaded shelter

Asphaltum n. a dark substance found in natural beds

Badger n. a burrowing animal

Band n. two or more extended families that lived together under one leader

Bark n. the outside covering of trees and plants

Bois d'arc (bwa dark) n. a yellow wood used by natives to make bows

Breechcloths n. a cloth worn around the body from the waist down

Bride service a Karankawa custom in which a newly marriage man give his father-in-law everything he gains hunting or fishing for an agreed upon period of time.

Buckskin n. the skin of a deer

Buffalo story hide a Kiowa history drawn and painted onto a buffalo hide

Bulb n. an underground bud that grows root from the underside

Caddi n. Caddo tribal chief or governor of a Caddo city-state

Campaign n. a series of military events for a special purpose

Cane n. a plant that has a long jointed woody stem

Cedar n. an evergreen tree

Ceremony n. a formal activity

Character n. a moral quality

Chief n. the leader of a group

Christian n. a person who believes in the teachings of Jesus Christ

Clan n. a group of people descending from a common ancestor

Club n. a heavy stick used as a weapon

Coast n. the land next to the sea

Coastal prairie a narrow stripe of land on the mainland of Texas

Comanchería n. the land of the Comanche

Cone n. a form with a circle at the base and a pointed top

Cremate v. to burn a dead body to ashes

Cross Timbers a mixed wooded area of Texas

Currant n. a small seedless berry

Deerskin n. the skin of a deer

Diameter n. the straight line passing through the center of a circle

Diet n. a choice of food

Ditch n. a long narrow hole dug in the ground

Dogwood n. a tree with pink or white flowers

Drought n. a long period of dry weather

Eagle dance a special Comanche celebration for a boy after his first successful hunt

Elk n. a large North American deer with spreading antlers

Environment n. surroundings that include physical, social, and cultural conditions

Extended family families that include grandparents, aunts, uncles, and cousins.

Fierce adj. violent in temperment

Flint n. a hard kind of stone

Fowl n. any of several birds

Gourd n. the fruit of various plants whose dried shell is used for bottles.

Granaries n. storehouses for grain

Great Plains an area of dry flat grassland

Great Spirit n. native's god

Guardian n. one who protects

Harshness n. cruelty

Herbs n. plants valued for their healing powers

Hickory n. a North American tree of the walnut family

Hollowed adj. having a space inside

Hunter-gatherer n. people who survive by searching for wild plants and animals

Iron point an arrow point made of iron

Jacale n. a small hut made of branches and mud

Javelina n. wild pig

Lagoon n. a small pond like body of water

Lance n. a long spear with a metal head

La Salle n. French explorer

Leggings n. leather covering for the legs

Lipan a band of Apache found on the south Texas plain

Lodge n. a shelter or hut

Loincloths n. a cloth worn around the body from the waist down

Maize n. corn

Marsh n. an area of low wet land

Medicine n. A Comanche's personal spiritual power

Medicine bundles Kiowa holy charm

Medicine man n. priest or holy person of native farming communities

Mel n. Karankawa god

Mescalero a band of Apache who lived in the mountains of west Texas

Mesquite beans the bean of a spiny shrub found in the southwest United States

Milling stones stones used to grind corn and grains into flour

Mistletoe n. an evergreen plant with white berries

Mitotes n. celebration held by the Gulf Coastal Natives

Moccasins n. heelless shoes made of soft deerskin

Mohawk a hair style where the head is shaved except for a strip in the center of the head

Mother Earth goddess of the earth, she allows or help things to grow

Mourning n. showing sorrow for a person's death

Mulberry n. a tree with dark purple berries that can be eaten

Muskmelon n. a round oblong melon

Network n. a linking of separate locations as in a trade network

Nomadic adj. to wander and have no fixed home

Osage-orange a tree common to the prairies of the southwest. It produced a hardwood use by natives to make bows.

Oval adj. egg shaped

Pallet n. a bed or mattress of straw

Palo Duro Canyon a deep valley with steep sides found in the Texas Panhandle

Pattern n. a mode of behavior

Peace pipe a pipe used in special Native ceremonies

Pendant n. a hanging ornament like a locket

Persimmon n. a plum like fruit

Pichini n. Karankawa god

Plain n. flat rolling land

Plains Jumano a group of semi-nomadic Texas Natives

Plateau n. area of high flat land that drops sharply on one or more sides

Plaza n. a public square

Poncho n. a blanket like cloak

Potter n. a person who makes pottery

Pottery n. ceramic, earthenware, and stoneware

Prickly pear a type of cactus

Primitive adj. simple

Proportioned adj. balanced

Pueblo n. flat roofed building made of adobe

Pueblo Jumano a band of agricultural Natives that lived in the Rio Grande River valley

Purification n. the process of making something or someone pure, a native religious rite

Quiver n. a case for holding and carrying arrows

Rank n. social standing or class

Ritual n. a special practice or activity usually religious

Sacred fire the continual fire in the temples of the Caddo

Seasoned adj. stronger or better for use

Shaman n. priest or holy man

Sinew n. tendon

Slavery n. the owning of slaves as a custom

Society n. a group of individuals living together in a community

Sotol n. a cactus found in North America

Spanish moss n. a plant that grows in the southern United States

Stamina n. having the power to bear work, tiredness, and so on

Sturdy adj. strong and healthy

Supernatural adj. outside what is explainable

Superstitious adj. act within irrational belief

Surround n. a hunting method used by some Native groups

Symbol n. a material object representing something

Tanned adj. treated to soften and waterproof

Tanner n. a person who tans hide as a their job

Thatch n. a plant material used for roofing

Tomahawk n. a light ax used by the Natives as a weapon

Traditional adj. an act, idea, legend hand down

Trapped v. a way of catching animals

Tribe n. a number of bands that follow the same leader and share the same culture and territory

Tuber n. an oblong underground growth, potato

Vegetation n. plant life that grows in an area

Vision quest a Comanche brave's ritual to find their "medicine"

Wild mustangs the descendents of the Spanish horses that live on the great plains

Willow n. a tree that have strong flexible branches

Xinesí (shenesi) n. a Caddo chieftain

GLOSSARY ONLY SOURCES

Anderson, Adrian N., Ph.D, et al. *Texas And Texans.* New York: Glenco McGraw-Hill, 2003.

Fehrenbach, T. R., Siegel, Stanley, Dr., Crowley, David. *Lone Star: The Story of Texas.* Glenview: Prentice Hall, 2003.

Plains Indians – the tanning process. 29 June 2005.<http://www.saskschools. ca/~regory/firstnations/tanning.html>.

Stien, Jess, ed. *The Random House Dictionary: Concise Edition.* New York: Random House, 1980.

Willoughby, Larry. *Texas!.* Austin: Holt, Rinehart and Winston, 2003.

ACKNOWLEDGEMENTS

I would like to thank a few people for their help and support in this effort. This book never would have happened without them. A very big thank you has to go to Millie Garrison for her editorial assistance. It is wonderful to work with someone you can trust. I couldn't ask for a better friend. Also, thank you to Gary Garrison. You kept me laughing throughout the process, made some editorial comments that were very helpful, but mostly put up with the hours of phone calls to your wife.

Finally, thanks to my publisher, Michael

Long, for always believing in what I can do

and just letting me do it.

Grace Stamper

ABOUT THE AUTHOR

Grace Stamper is a graduate of the University of Dayton, Ohio, where she earned a BS in Secondary Education/ History and Government Comprehensive. She obtained her Masters in Education with a minor in History from Sam Houston State University, Huntsville, Texas. Ms. Stamper has been teaching history for 30 years, and has taught in Aldine, Splendora, and currently in Magnolia, Texas as well as public and private schools outside of Texas. She is a trained Learning Styles Specialist, and has devoted her time outside the classroom to curriculum and staff development. Ms. Stamper has presented various staff development programs over the years in several districts, has authored or coauthored district curriculum, and has presented at various conferences. For the past several years, she has been a regular presenter at the Texas Middle School Conference.